FLY with English

B Pupil's Book

Frances Bates–Treloar
Steve Thompson

Bill

Sam

May

Sue

Max

Pex

Marshall Cavendish
Education

Let's Start!

Fly With English B has been developed to ensure that young learners build on the vocabulary and language skills acquired in Fly With English A. The **Pupil's Book** focuses on developing accuracy in reading, listening and speaking for a wider range of contexts in line with the learner's own development. Learning is consolidated through each language skill, so that learners develop a higher level of comprehension and critical thinking skills. The corresponding Workbook emphasises writing and provides focused practice and consolidation of the language items taught.

The Pupil's Book provides many opportunities for individual, pair and group work. Skills-focused activities help the learner use English fluently and confidently.

New words are introduced with pictures to facilitate learning.

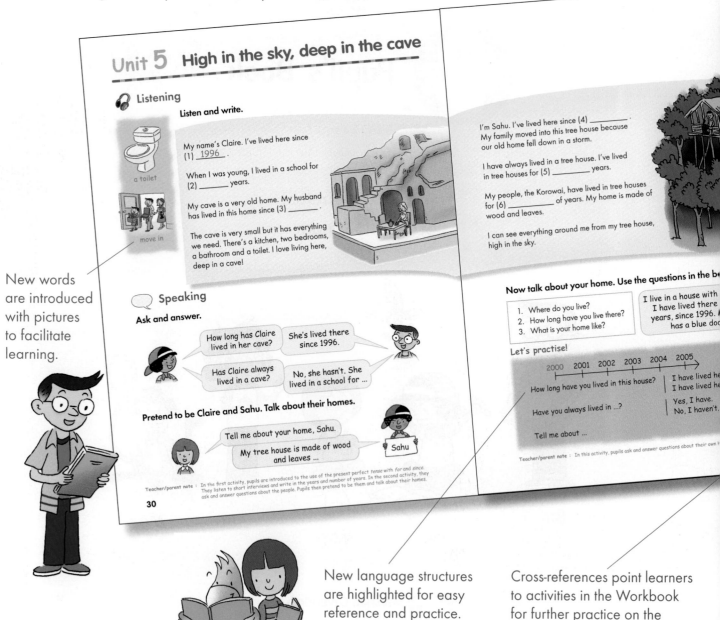

New language structures are highlighted for easy reference and practice.

Cross-references point learners to activities in the Workbook for further practice on the items taught.

ii

Language is presented and practised in real-life situations that offer meaningful opportunities for problem solving.

The teacher/parent note at the bottom of each page identifies the objective of each activity.

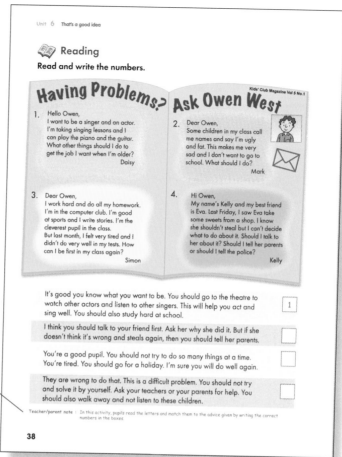

Unit 6   That's a good idea

Reading

Read and write the numbers.

Having Problems? Ask Owen West

Kids' Club Magazine Vol 5 No.1

1. Hello Owen,
    I want to be a singer and an actor. I'm taking singing lessons and I can play the piano and the guitar. What other things should I do to get the job I want when I'm older?
    Daisy

2. Dear Owen,
    Some children in my class call me names and say I'm ugly and fat. This makes me very sad and I don't want to go to school. What should I do?
    Mark

3. Dear Owen,
    I work hard and do all my homework. I'm in the computer club. I'm good at sports and I write stories. I'm the cleverest pupil in the class. But last month, I felt very tired and I didn't do very well in my tests. How can I be first in my class again?
    Simon

4. Hi Owen,
    My name's Kelly and my best friend is Eva. Last Friday, I saw Eva take some sweets from a shop. I know she shouldn't steal but I can't decide what to do about it. Should I talk to her about it? Should I tell her parents or should I tell the police?
    Kelly

It's good you know what you want to be. You should go to the theatre to watch other actors and listen to other singers. This will help you act and sing well. You should also study hard at school. `1`

I think you should talk to your friend first. Ask her why she did it. But if she doesn't think it's wrong and steals again, then you should tell her parents.

You're a good pupil. You should not try to do so many things at a time. You're tired. You should go for a holiday. I'm sure you will do well again.

They are wrong to do that. This is a difficult problem. You should not try and solve it by yourself. Ask your teachers or your parents for help. You should also walk away and not listen to these children.

Teacher/parent note : In this activity, pupils read the letters and match them to the advice given by writing the correct numbers in the boxes.

38

Revision units review and consolidate the vocabulary and structures taught. Activities are provided in assessment formats to develop the learner's confidence and facilitate the evaluation of outcomes.

Revision Unit 1

Reading

Read and answer.

KIDS' CLUB SCIENCE SHOW

Every summer holiday, *Kids' Club Magazine* has special programmes for children. This year's science show is called 'Life Fifty Years From Now'.

Find out about:

*   *Tomorrow's Robots*: When robots become cleverer than people, how will we use robots in our houses and factories?
*   *Offices in the Future*: What will people do in fifty years? Will we have to work? Listen to ideas about what jobs and office work will be like in fifty years.
*   *School and Learning*: Today's young teachers think pupils will learn from computers and will only speak to teachers by video or telephone from home.
*   *Food in Fifty Years*: The food we will eat in the future will be different from what we eat now. Learn what food will look like and taste like in fifty years.
*   *Sports and Hobbies*: Sports and hobbies have changed a lot in the last fifty years. What will they be like fifty years from now?

You can visit the Kids' Club Science Show at the Island Hotel every day from 9:30 a.m. to 6:00 p.m. The show will start on the 15th of July and will be on for three weeks. Phone Karl at *Kids' Club Magazine* at 6559403 for more information.

? What is the show about?

? What will be different in fifty years?

? When and where is the science show?

Now write yes or no.

1. Robots will be cleverer than people in fifty years' time.   yes
2. In fifty years' time, school children may learn most things from computers. _____
3. Food in the future will taste like the food which we eat now. _____
4. In fifty years' time, sports and hobbies will be the same. _____
5. You can go to the science show at the weekends. _____
6. The science show will end in September. _____

Teacher/parent note : In this activity, pupils read an advertisement and decide if the sentences about it are true or false.

42

Listening

Listen and circle the answers.

Hello! This is Karl at *Kids' Club Magazine*. Can I help you?

1. Ann: The camp starts next week, doesn't it?
    Karl: a) No, it starts in two weeks.
    b) No, you're wrong.
    c) Yes, it does.

2. Ann: What time should Ryan arrive?
    Karl: a) At 9:00.
    b) At 10:00.
    c) At 11:30.

3. Ann: What should he bring with him?
    Karl: a) Lots of money and food.
    b) Warm clothes and some food.
    c) Nothing. He doesn't need to bring anything.

4. Ann: He can play a lot of sports there, can't he?
    Karl: a) No, not very many.
    b) Yes, a lot.
    c) Only football and swimming.

5. Ann: And he's going to sleep in a tent, isn't he?
    Karl: a) That's right.
    b) Only for one night.
    c) No, he isn't.

6. Ann: Should I visit him?
    Karl: a) Yes, that's a good idea.
    b) Usually, we say 'no'.
    c) Perhaps.

7. Ann: Will Ryan enjoy the camp?
    Karl: a) Most children don't enjoy the camp.
    b) I don't think he will.
    c) Yes, I'm sure he will.

Now, ask and answer.

The camp starts next week, doesn't it?

No, it starts in two weeks.

Ann   Karl

Teacher/parent note : In the first activity, pupils listen to a conversation and circle the answers. In the second activity, they ask and answer questions from the first activity.

43

31

Contents

Structures	Functions
Question tags in simple present tense, present continuous tense and present perfect tense	Obtaining, understanding and checking information Giving personal information
Pronouns and adverbs to refer to unspecified people, places and things Infinitives to express purpose	Talking about unspecified people, places and things Describing personal and workplace activities and routines
Verbs *will, may, might* and *won't* for expressing probability and predicting things	Talking about probability and predictions about life in the future
Verbs of sensation + *like* + nouns to describe food and other things	Talking about and comparing how things taste, feel, sound and look
Present perfect tense with *for* and *since* to express duration of time Simple present tense with *ago* to talk about when something happened	Talking about how long a present action or state has been going on for
Giving suggestions and advice of different degrees using modal verbs *should, could* and structures *how about* and *why don't* Reinforcement of *will*	Giving suggestions and advice for everyday problems
Past continuous tense and *when* to express interrupted past states Reinforcement of modal verb *should* in positive and negative forms	Describing and narrating interrupted past events Setting a scene
Structure *will have to* to express future obligations or intentions Reinforcement of *before* Expressing the location of an activity or event using *where*	Expressing future intentions and obligations Talking about the location of an activity or event
Adverbs *too ...* and *not ... enough* to express excess and insufficiency	Talking about the excess and insufficiency of things to express satisfaction and dissatisfaction
First conditional *If..., will ...*	Expressing what will happen if a condition is met
Adverbs *too many, too much, a few* and *a little to* express excess and insufficiency	Talking about the excess and insufficiency of things to express satisfaction and dissatisfaction
Reinforcement of structures *going to, should, make* and *will* Reinforcement of first conditional *If ..., will ...*	Expressing ideas to achieve a goal Reporting past events

Reading

Read and answer.

a journalist

an artist

a detective

a writer

an envelope

✳ SUNSHINE TV ✳

Sunshine TV wants your help!

Sunshine TV is having a competition to find the best idea for a new children's TV programme.

WHAT DO YOU HAVE TO DO?
Think of an idea for an exciting and fun new programme for children.
Send a letter or an email with your idea before the 27th of April to:

Julia Foster
Sunshine TV
New Programme Ideas
Post Office Box 3149
TVideas@SunshineTV.com

WIN ALL THESE EXCELLENT PRIZES

- A visit to a TV studio
  - Meet a journalist, a famous artist and a writer
  - Interview a famous clown
- A video camera for your school

We've got a letter from Sunshine TV!

Quick, open the envelope! Have we won?

1st May

Dear Bill, May, Sue and Sam,

Thank you for your letter. I like your idea very much! I think children will enjoy watching a programme about young detectives who solve mysteries about missing pets.

Come visit us at Sunshine TV. My secretary will phone you soon to tell you more.

Yours sincerely,

Julia Foster

1. What is the competition for?
2. Where does Julia Foster work?
3. What is inside the envelope?
4. What do pet detectives do?
5. What prizes have the children won?

Teacher/parent note : Pupils read different texts for information and then answer questions about them.

6

 **Listening**

Listen, look and write the times.

1.

`8 : 00`

2.

`  :  `

3.

`  :  `

4.

`  :  `

5.

`  :  `

6.

`  :  `

7.

`  :  `

Check the times. Ask and answer.

The car arrives at 8:45, doesn't it?

Yes, it does.

We're going to interview Capo at 2:15, aren't we?

No, we aren't.

Let's practise!

... doesn't it?
... aren't we?

Teacher/parent note : In the first activity, pupils listen to a schedule, look at the pictures and write the times for each event. In the second activity, pupils ask and answer questions to check when each event is scheduled to take place.

Reading page 6 ➤ Writing page 7 ➤

Listening

Listen and tick (✓) or cross (✗).

a photographer

a tennis player

1.	Pablo is only famous for his paintings.	✗
2.	Julia thinks Pablo is an excellent photographer.	
3.	Pablo has one child.	
4.	Pablo lives in a big house.	
5.	Pablo is kind to his pets.	
6.	Pablo used to live in England.	
7.	Pablo is going to paint a picture of the studio.	
8.	Pablo doesn't like reading mystery books.	
9.	Teresa is married to a tennis player.	
10.	Pablo paints animals and photographs people.	
11.	Pablo and Teresa like each other.	

Teacher/parent note : Pupils listen to an interview and then decide whether the statements are true or false.

 **Reading**

Read and write yes or no.

The children looked excitedly around the circus for Capo. Bill saw a young man with curly brown hair. He ran up to him and asked, "Excuse me, is your name Capo?"
"No, it isn't. It's Ben. I look after the elephants. That's Capo there, the person with the big blue nose," he replied.

"You've got a big blue nose. You're Capo the clown, aren't you?" said Sue.
"Yes, I am. Hello, children!" said the clown with the big blue nose.
The children were surprised when they heard Capo speak.
"Gosh, you're not a man!" said May.
"No, I'm not. I thought everyone knew," Capo replied.
"We didn't know," said Bill.

"You have always worked in the circus, haven't you?" asked Bill.
"Yes, I have. When I first came to the circus, I sold ice-cream to the children. It was fun but I wanted to be a clown. Clowns make the children really happy. Every evening, they laugh and laugh. Clowns make the adults happy too. The circus is an interesting and fun place to be. Everyone is always smiling and laughing."

"You're happy, aren't you, Capo?" asked Sue.
"Yes, I am, I'm never bored here. But last week, my dog fell sick and died. I feel very sad. She was a friendly dog with a happy face. Her name was Bonnie."

"Would you like to come back to the TV studio with us, Capo? There's a dog at the studio with a happy face! You will come, won't you?" asked the children.

1. The children did not know what Capo looked like.   _yes_

2. The children were surprised because Capo is a woman.   _____

3. Capo has always been a clown in the circus.   _____

4. Capo did not like selling ice-cream.   _____

5. Capo likes being in the circus.   _____

6. Capo's dog is sad.   _____

Teacher/parent note : Pupils read a text and decide whether the statements are true or false.

Speaking page 8 ➤   Writing page 9 ➤

Reading

Look at the picture. Read and write the names.

footprints

a thief

Where did you last see Bongo?

In the basement. I left him there. I had a great idea for a new mystery book. I went to look for some paper ...

Sue
Bongo
Capo
Teresa
May
Bill
Sam

The four young pet detectives, Bill, Sue, Sam and May looked inside the big, dark and untidy basement at Sunshine TV. This was where Teresa left (1) _Bongo_.

The children looked everywhere for clues — things that would tell them where Bongo was. (2) _____ found a paintbrush with paint. (3) _____ found some big footprints. (4) _____ found a hat with plastic fruit on top of it. Some of the fruit had holes in them.

The children talked about what they thought happened to Bongo.

Sue said, "I think Pablo is the pet thief who has taken Bongo. Look at this paintbrush. I think it's Pablo's. Pablo has been here. Pablo likes animals, and he doesn't like (5) _____ because she sometimes forgets to feed Bongo."

Teacher/parent note : Pupils look at the picture, read the text and fill in the spaces with the names.

Sam thought the pet thief was someone else. "Look at these big footprints.

(6) _____ has got Bongo. She's sad and she wants a new dog. Bongo's got a happy face too, just like her dog."

(7) _____ said, "I don't know where Bongo is. But this looks like an important clue!" He pointed to some small pieces of plastic fruit leading to a cupboard at the back of the basement. Inside the cupboard ...

Now answer.

1. Why were the children in the basement?
2. What do you think happened to the fruit on the hat?
3. Who do you think has got Bongo?
4. What do you think was inside the cupboard?

Speaking

Look at the picture on page 10. Pretend to be the children. Where have they looked? Where are they going to look? Ask and answer. Use the words in the box.

next to	above	in front of	inside
behind	under	between	on

May, you've looked behind the clothes, haven't you?

Yes, I have.

Bill, you are going to look under the cupboard, aren't you?

No, I'm not.

Let's practise!

| ... haven't you? | Yes, I have.
No, I haven't. |
| ... aren't you? | Yes, I am.
No, I'm not. |

Teacher/parent note : In the first activity, pupils answer questions about the text. In the second activity, they look at the picture on page 10 again and ask and answer questions using the target structures.

Unit 2 Jobs for everyone

 Reading

Read and write yes or no.

a chemist

a postman

an office

a factory

a post office

a farmer

Jobs

Mr Lee : This week, we are learning about people and the work they do. You are going to talk to someone about their job. You can ask them anything about their job.

Sue : This is going to be interesting!

Mr Lee : You can talk to a postman or a chemist. You can go to an office, a shop, a factory — anywhere. Find out everything you can about the job you choose.

Sue : I'm going to talk to a postman about his job. That's easy because there are post offices everywhere!

Sam : Oh yes! There's a post office somewhere along Small Street. My Mum goes there to post letters and buy stamps.

Bill : What happens if we go somewhere and there's no-one there?

Mr Lee : Call the place before you go. Now, is everyone sure of what to do?

May : Mr Lee, there isn't anywhere I can find a farmer to talk to. I don't know anyone who is a farmer or where there are any farms. I have nowhere to go.

Mr Lee : You can think of someone else to talk to, May.

May : Can I see a dentist tomorrow?

Mr Lee : Yes. Do you want to learn more about dentists?

May : No, Mr Lee. There's something wrong with my tooth. It hurts!

1. The children are going to work in different jobs. ___no___
2. The children can speak to anyone about their job. _____
3. The children can go anywhere they like. _____
4. It is easy for Sue to find a postman to talk to. _____
5. Everyone is sure of what to do. _____
6. May wants to talk to a dentist about his job. _____

Teacher/parent note : This activity introduces pronouns and adverbs to refer to unspecified people, places and things. First, pupils read a conversation about jobs. They then read the statements and decide whether they are true or false.

Listening

Listen and write the words.

a footballer

rich

score

Yesterday, I met Marco, a famous footballer. I used a tape recorder when he spoke to me, so I could remember what he said. He told me he's (1) ___twenty-one___ years old this year. He has a house by the sea where he lives with his mother, father and brother. He's very (2) _____, but he gives most of his money to his family. There is nothing he can't buy!

Marco is also very clever. He liked school. He did well at (3) _____ and science but he was best at (4) _____. He can also speak (5) _____ other languages. He left school at sixteen and went to play for his football club. Last year, he (6) _____ fifty goals for his team!

Marco eats breakfast with his family every Sunday. Then he drives his brother to the sports club. His brother also wants to be a (7) _____ when he grows up. In the evening, Marco reads (8) _____ about sports. I think he's a great sports person!

Let's practise!

anyone	someone
anything	something
anywhere	somewhere
no-one	everyone
nothing	everything
nowhere	everywhere

Teacher/parent note : In this activity, pupils listen to an interview and complete Sam's article by writing the correct words in the spaces.

13

Reading page 12 ▶   Speaking page 13 ▶

Reading

a pilot

a mechanic

a doctor

an actor

a policeman

a newspaper

What do these people work as? Read and write the letters.

a. pilot	b. mechanic	c. chemist
d. doctor	e. actor	f. farmer
g. photographer	h. policeman	i. journalist

I fly planes to take people to different countries.

1.

I work in the hospital to help sick people get better.

2. _____

I work hard to catch thieves who do bad things.

3. _____

I use my camera to take pictures of people and places.

4. _____

I make medicine to help sick people get better.

5. _____

I grow vegetables and look after animals to sell at the market.

6. _____

I fix cars to make them move again.

7. _____

I write for newspapers and magazines to tell people the news.

8. _____

I act in films to be rich and famous.

9. _____

Teacher/parent note : In this activity, pupils read sentences with infinitives to express purpose and identify the jobs they describe.

 Listening

a fire station   smoke   a fire engine   a fireman

Listen and tick (✓).

1. Bill went to the fire station ...
    - ✓ in the morning.
    - ☐ in the afternoon.

2. Bill went there ...
    - ☐ to be a fireman.
    - ☐ to see a real fire engine.

3. The fire engine is red ...
    - ☐ to make it easy for other cars to see it.
    - ☐ to make it go faster.

4. The firemen drive ...
    - ☐ slowly to get to the fire safely.
    - ☐ fast to get to the fire quickly.

5. The firemen wear fire jackets ...
    - ☐ to protect them from the smoke.
    - ☐ to protect them from the fire.

6. It is dangerous for the firemen ...
    - ☐ to go into a burning building without water.
    - ☐ to go into a burning building without helmets.

7. Bill took a picture of the fire engine ...
    - ☐ to keep in his diary.
    - ☐ to show Mr Lee.

Teacher/parent note : In this activity, pupils listen to a conversation and tick the correct answers according to what they hear.

Speaking

Read and answer.

I'm Marco. I'm a footballer and I play football in competitions. I work at the football club and I have to wear a uniform to work every week. I have to play football on the field in all kinds of weather. I have also been to many interesting countries to play football.

1. Where does Marco work?
2. Would you like to be a footballer? Why? Why not?

Look at the pictures. Pretend these are your jobs. Ask and answer.

1.

What do you work as?

Where do you work?

What do you wear to work?

Do you go to different countries to work?

Do you like your job? Why?

2.

3.

4.

 What do you work as?

I'm a nurse. I help sick people get better.

One thing is the same for all the jobs. What is it?

Teacher/parent note : In the first activity, pupils read a text and answer some questions. In the second activity, pupils look at the pictures and ask and answer questions about the jobs. They then identify what the jobs have in common.

What do the children want their jobs to be like? Read and say.

Sue wants to work as a cook in a restaurant. She wants to work from 10:00 a.m. to 5:00 p.m., from Monday to Saturday. She wants to wear a uniform to work.

Where they want to work	Restaurant	Hospital	Studio	Sports school
Who/what they want to work with	Food	Teeth	Cameras	Children
Hours they want to work	10:00 a.m. to 5:00 p.m.	11:00 a.m. to 7:30 p.m.	1:00 p.m. to 4:00 p.m.	8:00 a.m. to 2:00 p.m.
Which days they want to work on	Monday to Saturday	Tuesday to Saturday	Thursday to Friday	Tuesday to Friday
What they want to wear to work	Uniform	Uniform	Beautiful clothes	Sports clothes

What do you want your job to be like? Why? Tell your friend.

I want to work as a cook in a restaurant.

I want to be a cook because I enjoy making good food for my friends and family to eat.

Teacher/parent note : In the first activity, pupils read the table and deduce from the descriptions what the characters want to be and what they want their jobs to be like. In the second activity, they talk about what they want their own jobs to be like in the future.

Unit 3 Our world in the future

 Listening

Listen and tick (✓).

1. How will sports be different in the future?

2. Which sport won't Sam play?

3. Who may not like the new sports?

Listen again. Ask and answer.

How will sports be different in the future?

People will have races in the air! Perhaps they will have races in space, too!

Teacher/parent note : This activity introduces the modal verbs *will*, *won't* and *may*. Pupils listen to a conversation and tick the correct pictures that answer the questions.

💬 Speaking

What will people do in the future? Look at the pictures and talk about them with your friend. Use the words in the boxes.

People will still swim in the water.

Perhaps people may swim with dolphins.

1.

will / water   may / dolphins
won't / sharks

2.

will / balls   may / shoes
won't / pick up

3.

will / films   may / living room
won't / cinema

Let's practise!

Will sports be different?   They may be different.
They will be different.
They won't be different.

Teacher/parent note : Pupils look at the pictures and use the helping words to formulate sentences using *will, may* and *won't*.

🎧 Listening

Listen and tick (✓).

Things which will be different in the future.

1. Pilots will fly faster and better planes. _____ ✓
2. Pilots will fly planes to other countries in seconds. _____
3. All policemen will wear everyday clothes to work. _____
4. Policemen will have better helicopters and cars. _____
5. Cooks will only cook vegetables and not meat. _____
6. There will be robots helping cooks in the kitchen. _____
7. Singers will know how to sing every song in the world. _____
8. The music that singers make will be very different. _____

Things which may be different in the future.

1. Pilots may fly planes that can go under the sea. _____
2. Pilots may live on planes. _____
3. Policemen may work in space too. _____
4. Every policeman may work with a robot dog. _____
5. Cooks may only have to cook once a week. _____
6. Cooks may cook in buses on the road. _____
7. People may decide what singers sing. _____
8. Singers may sing with parrots. _____

Teacher/parent note : Pupils listen to a conversation and tick sentences describing certain and probable future events.

 Speaking

Look at page 20 again. Ask and answer.

What **will** be different in the future?

Pilots **will** fly faster and better planes.

What **may** be different in the future?

Pilots **may** fly planes that can go under the sea.

What will be the same for these jobs in the future? Look at the pictures. Ask and answer.

1.  2.  3.  4.

What will be the same in the future?

Pilots will still fly planes to other countries.

What do you think will be different for these jobs in the future? Ask and answer.

What will pilots work with in the future?

I think they will work with robot planes which can become cars. Pilots can drive them to work.

Teacher/parent note : In the first activity, pupils revise the use of *will* and *may*. They ask and answer questions about the jobs on page 20. In the second activity, they look at the pictures and talk about them. In the third activity, pupils form their own opinions and say what will be different about the jobs in the future.

Reading

Today, we're reading about what the world will be like in thirty years' time.

Read and write the numbers.

1 In the future, we may live in very tall buildings made of glass and metal. Clever engineers will build very fast lifts to take us up the buildings. There will be parks and gardens on top of the buildings because there won't be space for trees on the ground.

2 We will go to different places faster by cars that travel in the air. Perhaps even the road itself might move! No-one will have to walk. But we won't be very healthy because we won't get enough exercise.

3 There will be computers in our homes which we will use to buy everything we need. We may not see our neighbours because we won't have to shop for weeks and we may not go out of our homes.

4 Children will study at home. They will learn everything on computers and they will talk to their teachers on video phones. Children might not have many friends because they won't get to meet many other children at school.

How people will work	5	Our health in the future	
How we will study and learn		How we will get from place to place	
Where we will live		Nobody knows what will happen in the future	
Where animals will live		Changes inside our homes	

Teacher/parent note : In this activity, pupils read short texts about the world in the future. They then match the texts with the correct titles.

5 In the future, more people will work at home. Also, machines and robots will do more work for us. This might make life worse because there won't be jobs for people who need them.

6 Life will be difficult for some animals. Every year, we will cut down more forests and jungles. We will grow food and build houses and offices where the animals live. There might not be anywhere for animals to live. We may only see them in zoos.

7 We will live longer because we will have better medicine. Cities and countries may then have too many people. There are some doctors who think there will be new and very dangerous illnesses.

8 In the future, some things may be better but some things may not. What will the world be like in thirty years' time? Nobody knows for sure.

Now talk about what will be good and bad about the world in the future.

The roads might move. No-one will have to walk.

But we won't be very healthy because we won't get enough exercise.

Let's practise!

Roads might move.
Children might not have many friends.

Teacher/parent note : In this activity, pupils talk about what will be good and bad about the world in the future.

Unit 4   The cooking competition

Reading

taste

smell

feel

Read and answer.

Cooking Competition
Friday, 12th May

Make healthy drinks and food for the new school restaurant!

The pupil who makes the best drink or the best meal will win free school lunches for a week!

1. What kind of competition is it?
2. What do pupils have to make for the competition?
3. What does the winner get?

Cooking Competition

What did the cook think? Read.

Pupil	What did they make?	How did it taste?	How did it look?	Other comments	Score
Bill	**Milk drink** Made with bananas, strawberries, milk and chocolate	4/5 Tasted lovely	3/5 Looked a strange brown colour	Strawberries made it smell very nice	**7/10**
Sue	**Fruit drink** Made with mangoes, limes and oranges	5/5 Tasted excellent	5/5 Looked very nice and fresh	Smelled lovely — I wanted more!	**10/10**
May	**Fish salad** Made with fish, rice, tomatoes and lime	4/5 Tasted very nice	4/5 Looked fresh and healthy but the fish looked dry	A good, healthy meal but didn't smell very nice	**8/10**
Sam	**Pizza** Made with onions, tomatoes, potatoes and chocolate	2/5 Tasted strange	4/5 Interesting — pizza looked like a star	Very heavy and hard — felt like a rock	**6/10**

Teacher/parent note : Pupils are introduced to verbs of sensation. In the first activity, pupils read a poster and then answer questions about it. In the second activity, they read a table for information.

Read the table on page 24 again and write the letters.

1. The cook thought _____d_____ tasted better than Sam's pizza.
2. The cook thought Sam's pizza looked better than _____.
3. The cook thought _____ tasted the best.
4. The cook thought _____ tasted the worst.

a. Sue's drink
b. Bill's drink
c. Sam's pizza
d. May's salad

 Listening

Who is the cook speaking to? Listen and write the numbers.

1

Listen again and tick (✓) or cross (✗).

1. May cooked the fish for thirty minutes. _____✓_____

2. May put one lime in her salad. _____

3. Sam wanted to name his pizza after Mr Lee. _____

4. Sue put two mangoes in her fruit juice. _____

5. Bill put chocolate milk in his drink. _____

Let's practise!

tasted	felt
smelled	looked

Teacher/parent note : In the first activity, pupils read the table on page 24 and complete the sentences. In the second activity, they listen and write numbers to indicate which character the cook is talking to. In the third activity, they listen again and decide if the sentences are true or false.

Reading

Read and answer.

Kids' Club Magazine 20th May

sound

I won the cooking competition in school and the cook invited me to the new school restaurant. The new restaurant was great but it sounded like a playground because twenty pupils were there. They were helping to paint the walls.

When I arrived at the kitchen, the cook gave me a cook's uniform. The hat was very thin and it felt like paper. It fell off my head many times! The cook taught me how to make different kinds of burgers. The best burger we made was the vegetable burger. It was made with vegetables but it tasted like meat.

The cook also taught me how to make some soup but I didn't like the soup. It looked like milk and smelled like fish. The last and best thing I made was a delicious dessert with mangoes and strawberries.

It was interesting to watch people work in the kitchen. It was very noisy when they were making the food, too. It sounded like a market in there!

After cooking, we had to wash up. The cook said, "As a cook, you have to do boring jobs, too!" He sounded like my mum. But I think I want to be a cook when I grow up. I don't enjoy washing the dirty plates but I love making nice food and drinks!

1.   Who invited Sue to the school restaurant?
2.   What food did she like the most?
3.   What did it sound like in the restaurant? Why?
4.   What didn't she like about being a cook?
5.   Did she enjoy visiting the school restaurant? Why?

Teacher/parent note : In this activity, pupils read the text and then answer the questions.

Speaking

Look at page 26 again. Underline the words looked like, sounded like, felt like, tasted like **and** smelled like. **Ask and answer.**

What did it sound like in the new school restaurant yesterday?

It sounded like a playground.

Look at the pictures and talk about the new school restaurant. Use the words in the boxes.

| tasted like | smelled like | looked like | sounded like |

The cake looked like a rabbit.

The cake tasted like carrot.

1.

cake / rabbit / carrot

2.

tea / orange / lemon

3.

sandwich / pepper / pizza

4.

song / fire engine

Teacher/parent note : In the first activity, pupils look at the text on page 26 and pick out the verbs of sensation. They then use them to formulate questions and answers about the text. In the second activity, they talk about the pictures using verbs of sensation.

Listening

What did Sue buy? Listen and tick (✓).

1.

    ✓

2.

3.

4.

Teacher/parent note : In this activity, pupils listen to the recording and look at the pictures. They tick the correct pictures that indicate what Sue bought at the market.

💬 Speaking

Look at the pictures on page 28. What did Sue buy? Why?
Ask and answer. Use the words in the boxes to help you.

tasted	freshest
looked	softest
felt	best
smelled	nicest

Which fish did Sue buy?

She bought the red fish.

Why did she buy the red fish?

Because it smelled the freshest.

Look at the pictures. Ask and answer. Use each word in the box once.

sweetest	funniest	softest	nicest

Why did May buy the red flowers?

She thought they smelled the nicest.

1.

2.

3.

4.

Teacher/parent note : Pupils practise using verbs of sensation and superlatives. In the first activity, they look at page 28 again and say what Sue bought and why. In the second activity, pupils look at the pictures and say what the characters thought.

Unit 5 High in the sky, deep in the cave

 Listening

Listen and write.

a toilet

move in

My name's Claire. I've lived here since
(1) _1996_.

When I was young, I lived in a school for
(2) _____ years.

My cave is a very old home. My husband
has lived in this home since (3) _____.

The cave is very small but it has everything
we need. There's a kitchen, two bedrooms,
a bathroom and a toilet. I love living here,
deep in a cave!

 Speaking

Ask and answer.

How long has Claire
lived in her cave?

She's lived there
since 1996.

Has Claire always
lived in a cave?

No, she hasn't. She
lived in a school for ...

Pretend to be Claire and Sahu. Talk about their homes.

Tell me about your home, Sahu.

My tree house is made of wood
and leaves ...

Sahu

Teacher/parent note : In the first activity, pupils are introduced to the use of the present perfect tense with *for* and *since*.
They listen to short interviews and write in the years and number of years. In the second activity, they
ask and answer questions about the people. Pupils then pretend to be them and talk about their homes.

I'm Sahu. I've lived here since (4) _____.
My family moved into this tree house because
our old home fell down in a storm.

I have always lived in a tree house. I've lived
in tree houses for (5) _____ years.

My people, the Korowai, have lived in tree houses
for (6) _____ of years. My home is made of
wood and leaves.

I can see everything around me from my tree house,
high in the sky.

Now talk about your home. Use the questions in the box.

1. Where do you live?
2. How long have you lived there?
3. What is your home like?

I live in a house with my family.
I have lived there for nine
years, since 1996. My house
has a blue door ...

Let's practise!

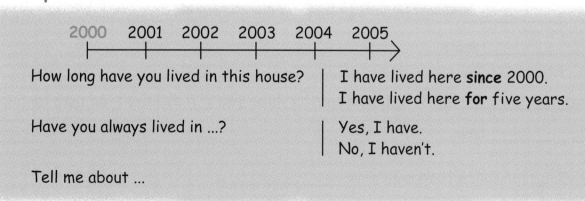

2000   2001   2002   2003   2004   2005

How long have you lived in this house? | I have lived here **since** 2000.
I have lived here **for** five years.

Have you always lived in ...? | Yes, I have.
No, I haven't.

Tell me about ...

Teacher/parent note : In this activity, pupils ask and answer questions about their own homes.

Listening

Listen and write.

an igloo

Third floor

__Mr__ and _____ Alberto have lived here _____ 1985. Their two children, Anita and Alfredo, moved away about _____ years ago.

Anita and Alfredo sometimes come back to stay for a _____ or _____.

Second floor

Mr and Mrs Short and their _____ children have lived here for _____ years. Mr Short has wanted to move to a house in the country for _____ years.

First floor

Mr and Mrs Kelly and their _____ children, one _____ and two _____ have lived here since _____. Next week, they are going to stay at their holiday house. Mr Kelly bought the house _____ years ago.

Ground floor

Mr and Mrs Raj, their three children, and Mr Raj's two _____ have lived here for _____ years. The Raj family went to the Arctic in 2003 for a holiday and stayed in an igloo for _____ days.

Now complete the sentences.

1. The ___Alberto___ family have lived here for the longest time. They have lived here for _____ years.

2. The _____ family has lived here for three years. They have lived here for the _____ time.

3. The Short family has lived here since _____ .

Teacher/parent note : In the first activity, pupils listen to a recording about Sam's neighbours and complete the sentences. In the second activity, pupils complete the sentences based on the text in the first activity.

 # Reading

Read and write yes or no.

Tell us more about yourself, Claire!

In 1970, I was born in a small town in New Zealand. For fourteen years, I lived in a school that belonged to my grandparents. I had many friends to play with there.

In 1988, when I was eighteen years old, I moved to Australia. I studied business at university for three years. After university, I worked very hard for a few years and made a lot of money. But I got tired of working long hours, so my friend and I decided to go on a holiday around the world and have a great adventure!

After visiting many countries, I came to Turkey in 1995. I met my husband, fell in love and got married. We often go to weddings and parties. I went to a wedding two days ago. My husband's cousin got married to his girlfriend. They went out for two years.

Now, I have a shop that sells all kinds of colourful carpets. Tomorrow, I am going to New Zealand for seven weeks to visit my family! I haven't been back there for seven years.

I have had an interesting life since I moved to Turkey ten years ago. I love my home in a cave and I love the Turkish people. I will stay here for the rest of my life.

1. Claire lived in her grandparents' school fourteen years ago.   _____no_____

2. Claire studied in Australia for three years.   _____

3. Claire has not lived in New Zealand since 1995.   _____

4. Claire's husband's cousin got married two years ago.   _____

5. Claire often goes back to New Zealand.   _____

Let's practise!

1995 1996 1997 1998 1999 2000 2001 2002 2003 2004 2005 ⟶

In 1995, I moved to Turkey.
I moved to Turkey ten years ago.

Teacher/parent note : In this activity, pupils read the text and then decide if the statements are true or false.

Reading

Read and circle the answers.

a ladder

Do you know that I had a tree house too, May?

Tell me about it, Dad.

A long time ago, before you were born, I used to have a tree house. My father built it for my brother and me. It was made of old wood that my dad found in the garden. The garden had many trees. Some of the trees have been there since 1901.

My tree house was up in a big tree. It had glass windows, small plastic chairs for us to sit on and a table to put our food. My brother and I got up to the tree house by climbing a ladder. A ladder helps us get to places that are high.

Our neighbour's son, Ethan, came to play in my tree house, too. We met when we were three years old. He was my best friend thirty years ago. He's still my best friend. He moved to Turkey three months ago.

The three of us played in the tree house for eight years. Then we got too big for our tree house. My favourite toy lived up in the tree house, too, my teddy bear, Mr B. He now lives in a cardboard box in our basement here! He's lived there since 1993, when your mum moved in!

1. Who built the tree house?

   a. Ethan's dad   b. May's grandfather   c. May's dad

2. Who is Ethan?

   a. May's uncle   b. May's best friend   c. May's dad's neighbour

Teacher/parent note : Pupils read a text and review *for*, *since* and *ago* and then answer multiple choice questions.

3. How long has May's dad known Ethan?

   a. three months   b. three years   c. thirty years

4. Why did the three boys move out of the tree house?

   a. Ethan moved to Turkey.   b. They got too big.   c. May's mum moved in.

5. When did Mr B move to the basement?

   a. 1993 years ago   b. since 1993   c. in 1993

 ## Speaking

Find out about your friend. Ask and write. Use the words in the box to help you.

where	how long
who	what

Where do you live, Sue?

My friend's name is _____		
	Lives in ...	**Has lived here for / since ...** (or has always lived here?)
	Best friend is ...	**Have been friends for / since ...**
	Favourite thing / toy is ...	**Has had it since / for ...**

Now talk about your friend. Use since **and** for.

 My friend Sue lives in a house in a big town. She has lived there for two years. Her best friend is May. They have been best friends since 1996.

Teacher/parent note : Pupils revise the present perfect tense to find out and talk about their friends.

Unit 6 That's a good idea

 Listening

Listen and write the letters.

Should I add chocolate when I cook dinner for my mother? It'll make the food more delicious.

No, you shouldn't. You should bake her a birthday cake.

a. It will make the food more delicious.　　b. It will make the room interesting.

c. It will make her angry.　　　　　　　　　d. It will make her happy.

e. It will make the floor wet.　　　　　　　f. It will make her ill.

1.  a

2.

3.

4.

5.

6.

Teacher/parent note : This activity introduces *It will ...*, *should* and *shouldn't*. Pupils listen to a conversation and match the sentences to the correct pictures.

Who had these ideas? Listen and write M for May, B for Bill or S for Sam.

curtains

1. Sue should paint the walls blue.   _____B_____

2. Sue should buy a bigger bed.   _____

3. Sue should put more flowers and plants in her room.   _____

4. Sue should change the curtains on her windows.   _____

5. Sue should put a TV and an armchair in her room.   _____

6. Sue should put more mirrors in her room.   _____

Do you agree with their ideas? Why? Use the words in the box to help you.

boring
smaller
more interesting
more beautiful
more comfortable
brighter
cooler
fresher
bigger

Yes, Sue should paint the walls blue. It'll make the room feel cooler.

Let's practise!

It will It'll	make ...
She	should ... shouldn't ...

Teacher/parent note : Pupils practise using *should* and *shouldn't*. In the first activity, pupils listen to a conversation and match the ideas to the characters. In the second activity, pupils say why they agree or disagree with the suggestions.

 # Reading

Read and write the numbers.

Having Problems? Ask Owen West

Kids' Club Magazine Vol 5 No.1

1. Hello Owen,
I want to be a singer and an actor. I'm taking singing lessons and I can play the piano and the guitar. What other things should I do to get the job I want when I'm older?
Daisy

2. Dear Owen,
Some children in my class call me names and say I'm ugly and fat. This makes me very sad and I don't want to go to school. What should I do?
Mark

3. Dear Owen,
I work hard and do all my homework. I'm in the computer club. I'm good at sports and I write stories. I'm the cleverest pupil in the class.
But last month, I felt very tired and I didn't do very well in my tests. How can I be first in my class again?
Simon

4. Hi Owen,
My name's Kelly and my best friend is Eva. Last Friday, I saw Eva take some sweets from a shop. I know she shouldn't steal but I can't decide what to do about it. Should I talk to her about it? Should I tell her parents or should I tell the police?
Kelly

It's good you know what you want to be. You should go to the theatre to watch other actors and listen to other singers. This will help you act and sing well. You should also study hard at school.	1
I think you should talk to your friend first. Ask her why she did it. But if she doesn't think it's wrong and steals again, you should tell her parents.	
You're a good pupil. You should not try to do too many things at a time. You're tired. You should go for a holiday. I'm sure you will do well again after that.	
They are wrong to do that. This is a difficult problem. You should not try and solve it by yourself. Ask your teachers or your parents for help. You should also walk away and not listen to these children.	

Teacher/parent note : In this activity, pupils read the letters and match them to the advice given by writing the correct numbers in the boxes.

Look at page 38 again. What did Owen West say they should do? Tick (✓) or cross (✗).

1. Mark should forget about what the children did and not tell anyone.   ✗ _____

2. Simon should go on a holiday.   _____

3. Kelly should not tell her friend's parents anything.   _____

4. Daisy should not try to be a singer and actress. She should just study hard.   _____

💬 Speaking

Do you agree with Owen's advice? Say why.

I agree with Owen's advice to Daisy. Daisy should watch and listen to singers and actors. She will learn to sing and act better.

I don't agree with Owen's advice to Daisy. Daisy shouldn't go to theatres too often because she will need a lot of money. She can watch actors and listen to singers on TV.

Which person has the easiest problem to solve? Which person has the most difficult problem to solve? Why?

I think ... has the easiest problem to solve because ...

I think ... has the most difficult problem to solve because ...

Teacher/parent note : In the first activity, pupils read the advice on page 38 again and decide if the statements about it are true or false. In the second activity, pupils say whether they agree with the advice given and state their reasons. They then say which they think is the easiest and the most difficult problem, and why.

 Reading

| an air conditioner | a water cooler | a fridge | plant | shade |

Read.

We often get hot and thirsty in the classroom. We're having a meeting to solve this problem.

Sue Why don't we have darker glass for the classroom windows?

May I think we should have a water cooler outside the classroom.

We should plant a big tree outside our classroom.
Sam

Why don't we have more fans in the classroom?
Mr Tyson

Why don't we get an air conditioner?
Mrs Yan

Why don't we just open all the doors and windows?
Mr Lee

How about having a fridge with bottles of water in the classroom?
Bill

There are lots of ideas, aren't there? Some ideas are better than others.

Teacher/parent note :   This activity introduces the structure *Why don't we ...?* to make suggestions. Pupils read the characters' ideas for solving a problem.

Whose ideas are these? Read page 40 again and write the names.

This is a good idea because ...

Mr Lee

1. it's very easy and you don't need any money. _____

2. it will cool the room very quickly. _____

3. it will cost less money than an air conditioner. _____

4. we will have bottles of cool water to drink. _____

5. there will be shade for the classroom. _____

6. it will help keep out the strong sun. _____

7. we will have cool water to drink just outside the classroom. _____

This may not be a good idea because ...

1. the wind might blow our paper around the classroom. _____

2. it will take a long time to grow. _____

3. the rain may come in through the windows and wet the floor. _____

4. it will take up a lot of space in the classroom. _____

5. the classroom may be too dark. _____

6. we will have to leave the classroom to drink water. _____

7. it costs a lot of money. _____

💬 Speaking

Talk about the ideas. What's good and bad about them?

We should have darker glass for the windows. The glass will help keep out the hot sun and keep the room cool.

Yes, but the room may also be too dark.

Let's practise!

Why don't we ...?

Which do you think is the best and the worst idea? Tell your friend why you think so.

Teacher/parent note : In the first activity, pupils match the ideas with the arguments for and against them. In the second activity, they practise making arguments for and against the ideas. They then decide which ideas are the best and worst and give their reasons.

Revision Unit 1

 **Reading**

Read and answer.

KIDS' CLUB SCIENCE SHOW

Every summer holiday, *Kids' Club Magazine* has special programmes for children. This year's science show is called 'Life Fifty Years From Now'.

Find out about:

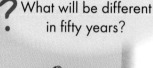 **?** What is the show about?

- *Tomorrow's Robots*: When robots become cleverer than people, how will we use robots in our houses and factories?
- *Offices in the Future*: What will people do in fifty years? Will we have to work? Listen to ideas about what jobs and office work will be like in fifty years.

? What will be different in fifty years?

- *School and Learning*: Today's young teachers think pupils will learn from computers and will only speak to teachers by video or telephone from home.
- *Food in Fifty Years*: The food we will eat in the future will be different from what we eat now. Learn what food will look like and taste like in fifty years.
- *Sports and Hobbies*: Sports and hobbies have changed a lot in the last fifty years. What will they be like fifty years from now?

? When and where is the science show?

You can visit the Kids' Club Science Show at the Island Hotel every day from 9:30 a.m. to 6:00 p.m. The show will start on the 15th of July and will be on for three weeks. Phone Karl at *Kids' Club Magazine* at 6559403 for more information.

Now write yes or no.

1. Robots will be cleverer than people in fifty years' time.   _yes_

2. In fifty years' time, school children may learn most things from computers.   _____

3. Food in the future will taste like the food which we eat now.   _____

4. In fifty years' time, sports and hobbies will be the same.   _____

5. You can go to the science show at the weekends.   _____

6. The science show will end in September.   _____

Teacher/parent note : In this activity, pupils read an advertisement and decide if the statements about it are true or false.

 **Listening**

Listen and circle the answers.

Hello! This is Karl at
Kids' Club Magazine.
Can I help you?

1. Ann: The camp starts next week, doesn't it?
   Karl: a) No, it starts in two weeks.
   b) No, you're wrong.
   c) Yes, it does.

2. Ann: What time should Ryan arrive?
   Karl: a) At 9:00.
   b) At 10:00.
   c) At 11:30.

3. Ann: What should he bring with him?
   Karl: a) Lots of money and food.
   b) Warm clothes and some food.
   c) Nothing. He doesn't need to bring anything.

4. Ann: He can play a lot of sports there, can't he?
   Karl: a) No, not very many.
   b) Yes, a lot.
   c) Only football and swimming.

5. Ann: And he's going to sleep in a tent, isn't he?
   Karl: a) That's right.
   b) Only for one night.
   c) No, he isn't.

6. Ann: Should I visit him?
   Karl: a) Yes, that's a good idea.
   b) Usually, we say "no".
   c) Perhaps.

7. Ann: Will Ryan enjoy the camp?
   Karl: a) Most children don't enjoy the camp.
   b) I don't think he will.
   c) Yes, I'm sure he will.

Now, ask and answer.

The camp starts next week, doesn't it?

No, it starts in two weeks.

Ann   Karl

Teacher/parent note : In the first activity, pupils listen to a conversation and circle the answers. In the second activity, they ask and answer questions from the first activity.

Speaking

Look at the pictures. Pretend to be Ryan. Ask and answer. Use the questions in the box to help you.

 Who's your best friend, Ryan?

My best friend is John.

 Ryan

1.
John
Ryan

Who's your best friend?
When did you meet him/her?
Where do you go to school?
How do you get there?
Have you got a bike?
When did you get it?
Have you got a pet?
How long have you had it?

2.
LONDON BOYS' SCHOOL

3.

4.

Now ask and answer with your friend. Use the questions in the box above to help you.

 Who's your best friend, Sue?

My best friend is May.

Teacher/parent note : In this activity, pupils look at the pictures and revise *wh-* questions, *since* and *for*. They then ask and answer the same questions among themselves.

 Listening

Listen and circle. Then write the letters.

ok = ☺

Good = ☺

Very good = ☺

a. They should make the camp cheaper and better.
b. They should have better food next year.
c. I think they should have a better singer.

Hani

Camp	☺	☺	☺
Food	☺	☺	☺
Party	☺	☺	☺
Group	☺	☺	☺
Advice	b		

Ming

Camp	☺	☺	☺
Food	☺	☺	☺
Party	☺	☺	☺
Group	☺	☺	☺
Advice	___		

Daisy

Camp	☺	☺	☺
Food	☺	☺	☺
Party	☺	☺	☺
Group	☺	☺	☺
Advice	___		

Now ask and answer.

Hi Hani! What did you think of the camp?

I thought it was good.

Hani

Teacher/parent note : In this activity, pupils listen to interviews about the Kids' Club Summer Camp and complete the survey forms. They then ask and answer the same questions.

Unit 7 Sea monsters

 Reading

a turtle   an octopus   float   the environment   rubbish

Read and answer.

The sun was shining and there weren't any clouds in the sky. Bill was at the beach. He was studying sea animals at school and hoped to find some that day.

Bill was walking on some rocks by the sea when he saw some plastic bags floating in the water. Then, Bill saw something else floating with the plastic bags. It looked like a shiny grey rock. "But rocks don't float!" Bill thought.

Bill moved closer to look. The rock had a head, four legs and a tail. It was a turtle! He also saw that it had a plastic bag around its head and one of its legs. It was trying to eat the plastic bag. Bill wanted to help the turtle. When the turtle swam near the rocks, he tried to catch it. Suddenly, he slipped and …

? What happened to Bill?

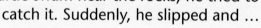

At the same time, a giant spotted octopus was trying to sleep in its underwater cave when suddenly there was a loud noise.

"What was that? It looks like a big fish, but it isn't swimming very well," thought the octopus.

? What do you think the big fish really was?

The octopus didn't want the fish to come near his cave, so it shot some ink into the water. The water quickly went black.

Bill felt weak. The water around him was black. He tried swimming up to the rocks, but he couldn't. He was slowly sinking when he heard a strange noise. It sounded like someone speaking. Then he saw something. "A sea monster!" he thought. But when he saw its eight arms and round head, he knew it was an octopus.

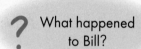

Teacher/parent note : Pupils are introduced to the use of the past continuous tense with *when* to express interrupted past states. In this activity, pupils read a story and answer the questions.

46

Then the octopus spoke to Bill. "Go away! I was trying to sleep when you disturbed me."

Bill was surprised that he could understand the octopus. "I'm sorry I disturbed you," said Bill. "But can you take me up to the beach, please?"

"OK, but don't come back!"

The octopus took Bill's hand with one of its long arms and pulled him quickly up to the rocks. "Thank you!" Bill said. The octopus waved its arms and swam away.

Bill climbed up on the rocks and looked around. The turtle was nowhere to be seen. The plastic bags were now floating nearer the rocks. Bill reached into the sea and picked them up. "I should put these in a bin," he thought. "People should take care of the environment! They should throw their rubbish in a bin, not in the sea. It can make the sea animals very sick and they could die. Then, they will be extinct!"

Bill was looking in the water for more plastic bags when he saw a long green fish. "Hello!" he said. The fish swam away. Bill laughed. "I can't speak to animals after all!" he said to himself. "Was it a dream?" But his hair and clothes were wet, and his arm was hurting.

Bill never told anyone about that day. It was his secret. He didn't want people to laugh at him. They wouldn't believe him. He often went to the sea, sometimes to swim, sometimes to fish, and sometimes to look for the spotted octopus. But he never saw it again.

? Why didn't Bill tell anyone about the octopus?

1. What was Bill hoping to find at the beach? Why?

2. What was Bill trying to do when he fell into the sea?

3. What was the octopus doing when it heard the loud noise?

4. What was making the noise? What was happening?

5. How did Bill know it was not a dream?

Let's practise!

The sun **was shining**.
Bill **was walking** on some rocks by the sea **when** ...

Teacher/parent note : Pupils answer questions about the story they have read.

Reading

a ship

Read and write the letters.

Do you believe in sea monsters? I was reading some old newspapers when I found these interesting stories.

a. was sailing	b. was coming	c. was watching
d. was sitting	e. was swimming	f. was looking
g. were playing	h. were fishing	

1. It was a lovely summer day in 1961. Many people were enjoying a day out at the beach. Mr Green __d__ on the sand with his wife, eating a sandwich. His children _____ noisily near the water, when they suddenly saw something strange in the sea. It _____ out of the water when Mrs Green screamed loudly. The horrible monster looked at them and quickly swam back into the sea.

2. It was the 6th of August 1948. Seven men were sailing on the ship 'The Daedalus'. One of the men _____ sea birds, when he saw a very long animal in the water near the ship. It _____ with its head above the water. The man quickly called out to his friends to come and look at the animal. After that, people often sailed there from far away places, hoping to see the strange animal.

3. Robert Sam was a famous magazine photographer. In December 1920, he was on a holiday in Australia. He _____ in a boat with some friends. There were no clouds in the sky and the sea was clear. Robert _____ at the water, watching the turtles and pink dolphins, when he suddenly saw something very strange swimming near the boat! He shouted loudly in surprise. His friends, who _____, turned around to see what was happening. They quickly took some photos of the monster before it swam away.

Teacher/parent note : In this activity, pupils revise the past continuous tense by reading the stories and writing the correct letters.

48

Now read page 48 again and circle the answers.

1. Why did the monster that Mr Green saw go back into the water?
   a. It was afraid of Mrs Green's loud scream.
   b. It was afraid of the children playing noisily.
   c. It was tired.

2. Which part of the monster did the seven men see above the water?
   a. They saw its head.
   b. They saw its head and tail.
   c. They saw its body.

3. What was Robert doing at the time when he saw the monster?
   a. He was sleeping.
   b. He was taking some photos.
   c. He was watching the animals in the sea.

 ## Listening

Listen and write the numbers.

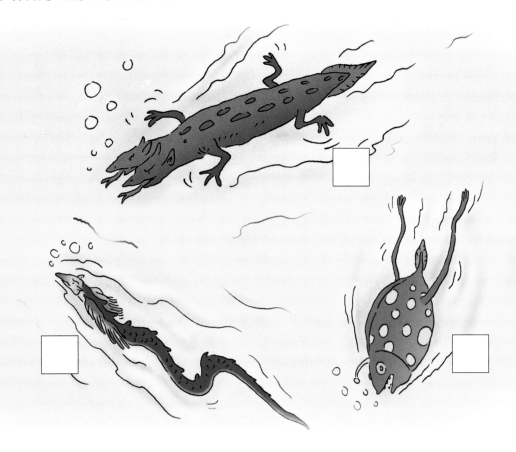

Teacher/parent note : In the first activity, pupils answer comprehension questions about the stories on page 48. In the second activity, pupils listen to short interviews describing different sea monsters and number the pictures accordingly.

 Listening

Listen and write the numbers.

Listen again and strike out the wrong words.

1. Mary was walking / ~~running~~ into the cinema when she fell and hurt her hand / leg .

2. Sue was looking for her tickets / sweets when she hit her head.

3. The young children in the cinema laughed / cried when the monster came out of the sea.

4. Mary was watching the film when she dropped her bag of chips / packet of sweets .

Teacher/parent note : In the first activity, pupils listen to a conversation and number the pictures accordingly. In the second activity, they read the sentences and strike out the wrong words.

Speaking

How can we look after the environment? What should we do? What shouldn't we do? Look and say. Use the words in the boxes to help you.

We should pick up rubbish so that children can enjoy swimming in the sea.

pick up	so that	clean play	enjoy build	swim

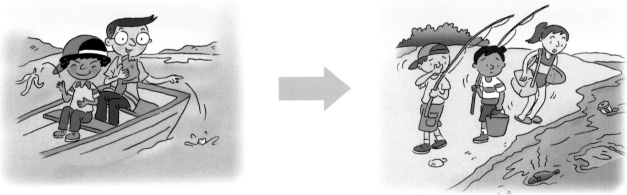

throw	because	dirty fish	die swim	smell

Teacher/parent note : In this activity, pupils revise *should* and *shouldn't*. They look at the pictures and talk about how and why they should protect the environment.

Reading

a police station   a doughnut   a key   midday   midnight

Read and answer.

It was a sunny Saturday in spring. Sue was sitting on the sofa reading. Mary was bored. She had a cold and had to stay inside. She wanted to go outside.

? What time is midday?

At midday, Sue heard the letterbox outside open and close. "Perhaps I've got a letter from Molly!"

"I want to come outside, too!" said Mary. "No, you can't. You'll have to do what I tell you," said Sue.

Sue ran to the letterbox and excitedly looked inside. Then, she heard a loud sound.

"Mary, did you close the door?" Sue asked. "Yes, it's closed. I brought the key. I put it in my pocket," said Mary. "MARY, that's the key to your doll house!"

"What are we going to do now?" whispered Mary. She was afraid. "We'll have to wait outside until Mum comes home," said Sue. "Sue, Mum and Dad might not come back until midnight. Will we have to break into the house? Will we have to sleep outside?" "Don't be silly, Mary!" said Sue. "I have an idea. Let's go to the playground at school. We can stay there until Mum and Dad come home."

"Sue, I want to see the tree frogs in Pets' Corner."
"You can't, Mary. I don't have the key to open the classroom door."
"We could look at the pets through the window," said Mary.
"No, we can't. My classroom is on the first floor," said Sue.
"Yes, we can. Look what I've found behind the bush!"

? What has Mary found?

"Mary, you can't climb up."
"Yes, I can. Look Sue, you'll have to hold it, and I will climb up."

"I don't see anything. There are no frogs!' said Mary.
"Don't be silly, there's Gus and ..." said Sue. Sue climbed up. Mary was right. The frog tank was empty.

"Follow me, Mary. Somebody has stolen our pets! I'll have to ask for help to find our missing frogs. Then, I'm going to phone the other pet detectives. We'll have to look for our pets and find out who the pet thief is!"

? Where do you think they are going?

"How are we going to get to the police station? We don't have any money for the bus. Sue, I'm hungry. I want a doughnut."

? How do you think they will get there?

Teacher/parent note : Pupils are introduced to the structure *will have to* express future actions. In the first activity, pupils read the text and answer the questions as they read.

Read page 52 again. Number the pictures in the correct order.

Now write yes or no.

1. Sue went outside to look in the letterbox.   _yes_

2. Pets' Corner is inside the classroom.   _____

3. Sue had money to buy Mary a doughnut.   _____

4. Sue and Mary were not at school because Mary was sick.   _____

Let's practise!

I You We	will have to ...	I'll You'll We'll	have to ...

Teacher/parent note : In the first activity, pupils number the pictures in the correct order according to the story on page 52.
In the second activity, pupils read statements about the text and decide whether they are true or false.

Listening

What will Detective Watson and Sam do next? Listen and write the numbers.

Listen and tick (✓).

1.   Who has a key to the classroom?

2.   Whose footprints might they be?

3.   What does the thief look like?

Teacher/parent note :   These activities reinforce the use of *will have to* and *might*. In the first activity, pupils listen to a conversation and number the pictures according to what they hear. In the second activity, pupils listen to another conversation and tick the correct boxes.

Reading

vitamins

Will the pet thief know how to look after Gus and Bud?

Do you have a book about looking after tree frogs?

Do you have tree frogs, Robert? Isn't your mother afraid of them?

Read and answer.

What is this text about?

White's Tree Frogs are found in Australia and Indonesia. They can grow as big as a baseball! They are bright green or blue in colour. They have special feet so that they can climb on slippery things. Before you get these interesting pets, there are some things you need to know.

The White's Tree Frog likes to eat crickets and other insects. It may not be easy to get food for your frog to eat. You will have to look for them outside, or even inside your home! You will have to catch a lot of insects or your frog will be hungry.

Next, you will have to give your frog vitamins to keep it healthy. You can buy vitamins from a pet shop or a vet in your neighbourhood.

You will have to keep your frog warm. But keep your White's Tree Frog away from the sun or it might die! You will have to wash your hands before you touch your frog. If you do not, your dirty hands could make it very sick.

Are you ready to begin? It is a lot of hard work to look after a White's Tree Frog, but it is lots of fun, too!

1. Are White's Tree Frogs easy to look after? Why?
2. What is special about White's Tree Frogs?
3. What will you have to do before you touch your frog?
4. Would you like to look after a pet frog? Why?

Let's practise!

before ...

Teacher/parent note : Pupils read a text reinforcing the structures *will have to* and *before*. They then answer questions about the text.

Listening

Listen and write the numbers.

Listen and write the numbers.

Pets' Corner

Now read and draw lines.

1. The library is where   •   •   Gus and Bud live.

2. The park is where   •   •   the children looked for Gus and Bud.

3. Pets' Corner is where   •   •   Gus and Bud are from.

4. Australia is where   •   •   Sam likes to go to think.

Teacher/parent note : In the first activity, pupils revise *after* and *before*. They listen to Sam talk about the order in which he is going to do things and number the pictures accordingly. In the second activity, pupils are introduced to the structure *where* to describe locations. In the third activity, pupils draw lines to complete the sentences.

Speaking

Look at the pictures. Talk about what happened. Use where and the words in the box to help you.

This is the bush where Mary found a ladder.

bedroom	classroom	bush

Gosh, the history test was difficult!

1.

2.

3.

Do you have a pet? If you don't, pretend you have one. Ask and answer. Use the questions in the box to help you.

1. What is your pet?
2. Where did you buy your pet?
3. What other pets can you find there?
4. Where does your pet come from?
5. What is special about your pet?
6. Where does your pet live?
7. What does it eat?
8. Where do you get its food?

PET SHOP
54 New Street

Let's practise!

The library is **where** Sam likes to go to think.

Teacher/parent note : In the first activity, pupils practise using *where* to talk about the location where something happened. In the second activity, they ask and answer questions about their pets.

Unit 9 Not too big and not too small!

 Listening

Listen and write the words. Use the words in the box to help you.

soft	expensive	high	heavy	big	small	tired

heavy

high

a trolley

a pepper

cheap

expensive

1 Can you fetch me two peppers please, Sue?

2 They're too ___small___.

3 They're not _____ enough.

4 That one's not _____ enough.

5 $8.50 They're too _____.

6 The shelf is too _____.

7 You're too _____ and too _____.

8 I'm not too _____ anymore!

Teacher/parent note : In this activity, pupils are introduced to new vocabulary and the structures *too ... and* and *not ... enough*. They listen to a conversation and complete the sentences with the correct adjectives.

Look at page 58 again. Read and write the letters.

a. tall	b. soft	c. hard	d. cheap	e. small	f. high	g. big	h. expensive

1. The pears are too __c__ . — The pears are not _____ enough.

2. The watermelon is too _____ . — The watermelon is not _____ enough.

3. The strawberries are too _____ . — The strawberries are not _____ enough.

4. The shelf is too _____ for Sue. — Sue is not _____ enough!

💬 Speaking

**Sue's family is at the supermarket. What is wrong? Look and say.
Use too and the words in the box to help you.**

heavy
expensive
low
soft
sour

$7.00

$10.00

Look, everyone!

The mangoes
are too soft.

Let's practise!

The mangoes are too soft.
The strawberries are not cheap enough.

Teacher/parent note : In the first activity, pupils complete pairs of sentences with the structures *too …* and *not … enough* using adjectives. In the second activity, pupils look at the picture and say what is wrong with the things in the picture using *too …*

Reading

 a cooker   hot chocolate   a marshmallow

Read and answer.

Soggy Fruit Juice Pasta with Eggs!

"Why are you cooking tonight? Where's Dad?" asked Sue.
"Your father is sleeping on the sofa! He's had a long day at work," said Sue's mum.

? What meal is Sue's mum cooking?

"Why are you putting the tomatoes in the bin, Mum?" asked Sue.
"Because they are too old and soft."
"But the pasta will be too dry without the tomatoes."
"Don't worry. I'll add some fruit juice and water," said Sue's mum.

"Mum, how long have you cooked the pasta?"
"Err … oh dear. I put it on the cooker at five o'clock. And now it's …"
"Half an hour! Mum, that's too long!"

? What time is it now?

"Let's put some eggs in, too."
"We can't put these eggs in the pasta. They aren't fresh. Look Mum, they're floating in the glass of water. This means they aren't fresh. Dad taught me this."
"Don't worry. Let's put the eggs in anyway," said Sue's mum.

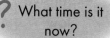

"Dinner time!" Sue's mum called from the kitchen.
A minute later, she came out from the kitchen and said,
"I'm sorry. I cooked the pasta for too long. It's burnt on top but it's too wet inside. It isn't good enough to eat. I'll give it to the chickens. Who wants to go to Doc's Café?"
"ME!" said everyone loudly.
"Hooray! No soggy fruit juice pasta that's just too horrible to eat!" sang Mary happily.
"The poor chickens," thought Sue to herself. "I'm sure they wish they could come to the café, too!"

"Don't worry, girls. Tomorrow night, I'll cook dinner as usual. After dinner, I'll make you all hot chocolate with marshmallows," said Sue's dad.

Teacher/parent note : In this activity, pupils read a text that reinforces the structures *too …* and *not … enough*. Pupils answer the questions as they read.

Now write yes or no.

1. Sue's mum cooks better than her dad.   ___no___
2. Sue's dad is usually too tired to cook dinner.   _____
3. The tomatoes were not fresh enough to use in the pasta.   _____
4. Half an hour was not long enough to cook pasta.   _____
5. The pasta was too dry.   _____

Now ask and answer. Use too and enough and the words in the boxes to help you.

Were the tomatoes good enough to use?

No, the tomatoes were too old and soft.

tomatoes / good / use
half an hour / long / cook / pasta
eggs / fresh / use
pasta / good / eat

Now talk to your friend. Ask and answer.

1. Are you old enough to cook in the kitchen?
2. Are you old enough to drive a car?
3. Are you strong enough to pick up a car?
4. Is your classroom warm enough to sit in without wearing a sweater?

No, I'm not old enough to cook in the kitchen. I'm just a child!

Let's practise!

The pasta will be too dry **without** the tomatoes.
Is your classroom warm enough to sit in **without** wearing a sweater?

Teacher/parent note : In the first activity, pupils read statements about the text on page 60 and decide whether they are true or false. They then ask and answer questions about the text using the structures taught. In the third activity, pupils ask and answer questions about themselves with their friends.

Listening

Listen. Tick (✓) and circle.

1. The music was ☑ too loud. very

2. The plate was ☐ too full. ☐ very

3. My stomach was ☐ full of vegetables. ☐ not full

4. There was ☐ too little pineapple juice. ☐ too much

5. The meal was ☐ not expensive. ☐ too

Listen again. Ask and answer.

1. Who liked the music in the café?
2. Who was happy with their meat and vegetables?
3. Who ate a lot of vegetables?
4. Who was unhappy with the waiters?
5. Will Sue's family go back to the café for another meal?

Teacher/parent note : These activities reinforce the structures *too ...* and *not ... enough* to express satisfaction and dissatisfaction. In the first activity, pupils listen to a conversation and choose the answers that describe what the characters thought. In the second activity, they answer questions about the conversation.

◯ Speaking

Look at the picture. Pretend you went to this café. What did you like? What didn't you like? Why? Talk about it. Use too and not enough and the words in the boxes to help you.

chairs	tables	waiters	fire	food	paintings

soft	warm	high	busy	noisy	colourful
hard	cold	low	empty	quiet	unusual

I thought it was an interesting place. I loved the chairs. I don't like very soft chairs and these were hard enough.

The waiters didn't speak or smile a lot but they were friendly enough.

Teacher/parent note : In this activity, pupils look at a picture of a café and read Sam's and Bill's opinions of it. Pupils then decide what they like and do not like about the café and talk about it using the adjectives and nouns in the boxes to help them.

Unit 10 If we have a party ...

 Listening

chopsticks   a spoon   a fork   noodles   Easter   a belt

Listen and write the numbers.

Must we invite Uncle Simon? ☐

Can your friends use chopsticks? ☐

What food are we going to have? ☐

How about playing football in the garden? ☐

Can we have an Easter party this year? 1

What games do you want for the party? ☐

Now answer the questions.

1. Who wears a belt and a striped shirt?

2. Who will have to use a fork and spoon to eat noodles? Why?

3. Why is it a good idea to play football in the garden?

Teacher/parent note : In the first activity, pupils listen to a conversation about a party and number the questions in the correct order. In the second activity, they answer questions about the conversation.

64

scold   turn off

Listen and write the numbers.

a. sings too loudly
b. is a good girl at the party
c. breaks something
d. is more friendly
e. brings his cat Rex
f. gives Bobby a cup of hot chocolate
g. eats too much ice-cream

1. If Uncle Simon _____d____, people will like him better.

2. If Bobby _____, Uncle Simon will scold him.

3. If Pex _____, Uncle Simon will turn off the TV.

4. If Mr Lee _____, Uncle Simon will go home early.

5. If Mary _____, Sue will phone her mum.

6. If Mary _____, she will get a new doll.

7. If Bill _____, Bobby will sleep better.

Let's practise!

If Uncle Simon is more friendly, people will like him better.

Teacher/parent note : In this activity, pupils are introduced to the first conditional. They listen to a conversation and then complete the sentences with the correct phrases.

Speaking

Look at the pictures. Complete the sentences in the boxes.

If Sam uses chopsticks, he will drop his noodles.

1.

Sam

If ..., he will drop his noodles.

2.

If ..., we can't play in the garden.

3.

Uncle Simon

If ..., we can't play noisily in the house.

4.

If we invite too many people, ...

5.

If Bobby gets a present, ...

6.

If Mary comes for the party, ...

Teacher/parent note : In this activity, pupils look at the pictures and complete the conditional sentences.

Look at the pictures. Ask and answer. Use the words in the boxes to help you.

What will happen if Mary pulls the dogs' tails?

If Mary pulls the dogs' tails, Bill will be unhappy.

1.

Bill

Mary

pulls / unhappy

2.

Pex

Uncle Simon

sings / shout

3.

Mum

Sue

breaks / call

4.

Uncle Simon

Mary

drops / scold

5.

Mum

Mary

is good / doll

6.

Mr Lee   Rex

Uncle Simon

brings / leave

Teacher/parent note : Pupils ask and answer questions about the pictures using conditional sentences.

📖 Reading

 poor

 Christmas

 a ghost

Read and answer.

A CHRISTMAS CAROL was written by Charles Dickens in the 19th century — more than 150 years ago. It is a story about a rich man, Ebenezer Scrooge, who loves money and is very unkind to others. The night before Christmas, the Three Ghosts of Christmas visit him. After their visits, Scrooge learns to be a better person. He becomes nicer to the people around him.

1. What is the name of the story?
2. Who wrote it?
3. What century was it written in?
4. Who is Ebenezer Scrooge?
5. What happens to him at the end of the story?

Read. Put the story in the correct order. Write the numbers.

What story are you reading, Bill?

I'm reading *A Christmas Carol*. The person in the story sounds like Uncle Simon!

That same night, a ghost visited Scrooge. It was his friend, Jacob Marley, who died seven years ago. "Scrooge, if you are horrible all the time, you will be like me when you die. I was a horrible person when I was alive, and now I have nowhere to go. But it isn't too late for you to change," said Marley. Marley left after telling Scrooge that three ghosts were going to visit him.

? Who was Jacob Marley? What did he tell Scrooge?

Teacher/parent note : In the first activity, pupils read a summary of a story and answer questions about it. In the second activity, pupils read parts of a story, answer the questions and number the parts in the correct order.

It was the night before Christmas. Fred invited his uncle, Ebenezer Scrooge, to Christmas dinner at his house but his uncle said "no" very rudely.

Scrooge was an unkind man who did not like people and did not have any friends. He even told poor Bob Cratchit, who worked for him, that he had to come to work on Christmas morning.

? What kind of man was Scrooge? | 1 |

Scrooge went out of his house. It was Christmas morning. After that, he was very friendly and kind to everyone.

Scrooge fell asleep. Suddenly, he woke up and saw the first Ghost of Christmas, who looked like a small, old man. The Ghost brought Scrooge back to the days when he was a boy. He showed Scrooge how Scrooge grew up to love money and nothing else. Scrooge was very sad at what he saw.

Scrooge went back to sleep. He woke up a second time and saw the second Ghost of Christmas, who was very big. He showed Scrooge people having Christmas dinners in their houses. Scrooge saw Fred and Bob Cratchit with their families. They were poor but happy.

After the second Ghost went away, Scrooge looked up and saw the third Ghost of Christmas. It looked like a dark fog in black clothes. Scrooge was more afraid than before. Together they went to a place and saw people talking about someone who had died. No-one looked sad. Everyone was happy. When Scrooge found out that he was the man who had died, he woke up.

? Who had died? Why were people happy?

Read and write yes or no.

1. If Scrooge did not change, he would become like Marley.   _____yes_____

2. Scrooge was good to Bob who worked for him.   _____

3. The first Ghost showed Scrooge what he was like when he was a boy.   _____

4. The third Ghost was a friendly ghost.   _____

5. In the end, Scrooge learnt to be a kinder person.   _____

Teacher/parent note :   In this activity, pupils read statements about the story and decide if they are true or false.

🎧 Listening

Listen and tick (✓).

	Too much	Too many	Not enough
Shorts		✓	
T-shirts			
Combs			
Chocolates			
Shampoo			
Soap			
Books			
Toothpaste			
Peanuts			

a suitcase

soap

a comb

shorts

shampoo

toothpaste

a peanut

a queue

Have you finished putting everything in your suitcase?

Oh dear!

Teacher/parent note : In this activity, pupils learn to use *too many* and *too much* and revise *not enough*. They listen to the conversation and tick the table according to the information given.

Listen and draw lines.

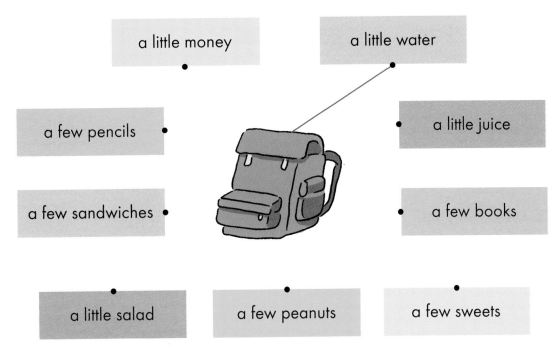

a little money

a little water

a few pencils

a little juice

a few sandwiches

a few books

a little salad

a few peanuts

a few sweets

Listen and strike out the wrong words.

1. There were too many / ~~a few~~ people in the queue.

2. There is not enough / too much apple juice for the children.

3. Betty drank a little / too much apple juice from Molly's cup.

4. Molly gave Michael too many / a few peanuts.

5. Betty ate a little / too much chocolate in the morning.

Let's practise!

too much	a few
too many	a little

Teacher/parent note : In this actiivity, pupils practise *too many, too much* and *not enough* with nouns. They also learn *a few* and *a little.*

 # Reading

a hostel   an airport   a swan

Molly's teacher is looking for a hostel in London. Read.

Green River Hostel

We have 150 beds.

- Students' rooms with eight beds: £16 a room
- Teacher's rooms with one bed: £7 a room

Each floor has a reading room and a games room. There's also a kitchen where you can cook your meals. We have breakfast every morning at our café at £5 for each person. Our computer room has 15 computers and it's open from 7 a.m. to 12 a.m. every day.

You can take a 20-minute bus ride to the city from the bus stop across the road.

Green River Hostel
10 South Hill Drive, London,
SW8 5EU England
Call us at 020 7400 5235

The Bridge House
138 — 142 High Bridge Road,
London, SW7 4ED, England
Phone us at 020 7222 4499

The Bridge House

A 3-minute walk to the west takes you to the bus stop with buses to the airport and the city. The nearest train station, King's Cross, is just a short walk away.

Have breakfast with us at £4 for each person. Our café is open from 6 a.m. to 11 p.m. every day.

What we have:
£14 a night for a room with eight beds
£22 a night for a room with four beds

There is a free newspaper for each of our 35 rooms every morning.

We also have a TV room, a reading room and a computer room with 10 computers.

Castle Park Hall

📞 Phone: 020 7480 0899
🏠 22A Castle Street, London, NE4 1JT England

Come stay with us!
Do you want to stay near East London's busiest streets?
We have rooms with eight beds (£18 a night for a room) for students
and special teachers' rooms with three beds (£20 a night for a room).

More about us:
- Email your family and friends any time you like! We have a 24-hour computer room with 5 computers.
- We also have a 24-hour TV room with video games.
- We are a 2-minute walk away from Marble Arch train station. From Marble Arch, walk straight on north to the famous Hyde Park and feed the swans in the Serpentine Lake.
- The bus stop is a 3-minute walk away.

Special breakfast at the Castle Park Café (7 a.m. – 11 a.m.) at just £3!

Now read Mrs Chang's list and tick (✓). Then add up the score for each hostel.

What we need	Score	Green River Hostel	The Bridge House	Castle Park Hall
Enough beds for seven boys, eight girls and three teachers	5	✓	✓	✓
Cheapest hostel	4			
Cheapest breakfast	3			
A short walk to bus stops or train stations	2			
About seven computers to write emails	1			
Score	15			

Which hostel has the highest score?

_____

Teacher/parent note : In the first activity, pupils read brochures about three hostels. In the second activity, they read the table and determine if the hostels have what Molly's teacher wants. They then add up the scores to find the best hostel.

Speaking

Molly and her friends went to many different places in London. Look at the pictures and talk about them. Use the questions and words in the boxes to help you.

1. Where did the children go? What did they do?
2. Do you think the children liked the places? Why? Why not?

They went to Hyde Park. Molly fed the swans bread.

I think Molly liked Hyde Park because there were many lovely swans to feed.

Molly	Robert	Sarah

fed	ice-cream	rode
swans	not enough	horses
lovely	expensive	friendly

Hyde Park

shopping	watched
too many	streets
people	interesting

Camden Market

waited	foggy
queue	far
too much	time

London Eye

Teacher/parent note : In this activity, pupils revise *too many, too much* and *not enough*. They describe the scenes by answering questions about the pictures using the helping words.

Unit 12 The new school garden

 Listening

a college   a pond   an umbrella   a swing   a butterfly

Listen and tick (✓).

1. What are Deepak and Sunni studying at college?

 ✓

2. What do Deepak and Sunni want in the garden?

3. Where are they going to put the pond?

Teacher/parent note : In this activity, pupils revise *going to* and *will*. They listen to a conversation and tick the pictures that answer the questions.

4. What will come to the garden if there are flowers?

5. What will make the garden cooler?

6. What are they going to need for a picnic?

 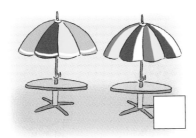 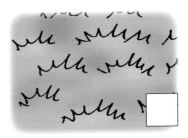

7. Which things are old and broken?

8. What is Mr Lee going to do?

Speaking

How are they going to help with the new school garden? Look at the pictures. Ask and answer. Use the words in the box.

What is Sue going to do?

Sue is going to paint butterflies on the wall.

| paint | put | catch | plant | make |

1.

2.

Sue   May

3.

Bill   Max   Sam

5.

4.

Teacher/parent note : In this activity, pupils look at the pictures and ask and answer about what the characters are going to do.

78

 # Reading

Read and answer.

 **THE SCHOOL GARDEN**

You have all done a great job with the garden. It looks beautiful. Well done!

We still need new swings and more tables and chairs for the garden. We would also like to have more plants and flowers.

We don't have enough money to finish the garden, so we want you to give us your ideas about how to collect more money.

Please write your ideas down and put them in the box in front of the school hall.

Mr Payton

1. What else does the garden need?
2. What ideas does Mr Payton want?
3. Why does the school need to collect more money?
4. What should pupils do with their ideas after they have written them down?

Here are the children's ideas. Read and draw lines.

If we sell flowers,	pupils and teachers will buy them to eat!
If we have a race around the town centre,	he might give us a picture to sell!
If we bake delicious cakes and biscuits and bring them to school,	a lot of people will buy them because they are so pretty!
There is an artist who lives in town. If we ask him,	people will give us money to run in an exciting competition!

Teacher/parent note : In the first activity, pupils read a notice and answer questions about it. In the second activity, they revise the first conditional by drawing lines to complete the sentences.

 **Reading**

Read and answer.

Our New School Garden
by May

12th October

? What was the old school garden like?

Four months ago, the school garden was a sad place where no-one went. There weren't any flowers and you couldn't hear any birds singing.

Then two college students, Sunni and Deepak, came to help us with the new school garden. They had many ideas. We planted flowers and trees and we put a pond in the garden so that insects, frogs, butterflies and birds would come.

? Where do you think the frogs live in the garden?

After working in the garden for two months, our new garden still wasn't finished. We didn't have umbrellas for the tables. We also needed new swings and more tables, chairs and plants. So we had to get more money to buy them.

? Why did they need umbrellas for the tables?

We had a race around the town centre. There were many people in town who loved to run. They gave the school money to run in the race. It was very exciting. A lot of people came to see who would win the race.

I also baked some cakes to sell at school. Sue baked biscuits, too. Sam made two tables so we didn't have to buy new ones. Soon, we had enough money to buy everything else that we needed for the school garden.

After another month of hard work, we had a beautiful new garden!

Yesterday, my friends and I had a picnic at the new tables. We enjoyed our lunch outside. We could hear the frogs in the pond and birds singing in the trees. There were many lovely butterflies flying around the flowers, and all kinds of fish swimming in the pond.

? Why did the children enjoy eating outside?

? What do you think a snack is?

Everyone at school thinks our new garden is great. It will be a lovely place to eat a snack at recess on a sunny day. Perhaps we will have some of our lessons there, too!

Teacher/parent note : In this activity, pupils read an article and answer questions about it.

Speaking

Look at the pictures. Tell the story of the new school garden. Use the words in the boxes to help you.

1 Mr Lee

wrote / jobs

First, Mr Lee wrote the jobs that everyone was going to do.

2 Max

planted / trees

3

collected / money

4 May

baked / cakes / sold

5 Sam

made / tables

6

bought / umbrellas / swings

7

finished / garden

Teacher/parent note : In this activity, pupils tell the story using the pictures and the words in the boxes.

Revision Unit 2

 Reading

Read and write yes or no.

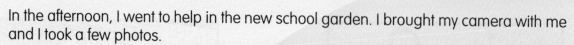

17th June

This morning, Mum gave me some money for helping to clean our bathroom and kitchen. Finally, I had enough money to buy the new camera which I have wanted for six months. I haven't spent any money since December.

I went to town by bus and Mum came with me. We went straight to the camera shop, and I bought the camera I wanted.

In the afternoon, I went to help in the new school garden. I brought my camera with me and I took a few photos.

First, I took a picture of two butterflies which were flying over the pond. Then I took a picture of Sam when he was sleeping under the tree. He doesn't know yet! I also took a picture of May when she was taking leaves out of the pond. There was a bird eating some food out of Bill's hand. Bill looked so afraid! I took a picture of him, too.

Mr Lee was also there. He was trying to make the robot pick up rubbish from the ground. But the robot was putting flowers into Mr Lee's mouth! I took a funny picture of them!

I'm going to put the photos in my dad's computer later tonight, and he will help me email them to my friends. I hope the photos will be OK. If they look good, I'll put them on the wall in my bedroom.

1. Sue spent all her money six months ago.   _no_

2. On 17th June, Sue had enough money to buy the camera that she wanted.   _____

3. Later that day, Sue took some photos in the school garden.   _____

4. The butterflies were flying over the pond when Sue took a photo of them.   _____

5. Sam woke up when Sue took a photo of him.   _____

6. Bill was feeding a bird when Sue took a photo of him.   _____

7. The robot was picking up rubbish when Sue took a photo of it and Mr Lee.   _____

Teacher/parent note : In this activity, pupils read a diary entry and then decide if the statements about it are true or false.

 **Listening**

Listen and circle the answers.

1. Sue: Oh dear. Here's the pond, but where are the butterflies?
   Sue's dad: (a) They're too small to see.
   b) They're in the corner of the picture.
   c) They've gone.

2. Sue: Look at the picture of Sam! What did I do wrong, Dad?
   Sue's dad: a) I think there wasn't enough light under the tree.
   b) I think his clothes were too dark.
   c) I think Sam was moving when you took the picture.

3. Sue: This photo of Bill is better, but we can't see Bill very well, can we?
   Sue's dad: a) No, we can't. There isn't enough light.
   b) Yes, we can. Bill is standing close enough.
   c) No, we can't. There are too many birds flying around.

4. Sue's dad: Look at Mr Lee! Why didn't the robot pick up the rubbish?
   Sue: a) The robot was too tall to pick up the rubbish.
   b) The robot wasn't clever enough to pick up the rubbish.
   c) The robot's arms were too short to pick up the rubbish.

5. Sue: There's too much sky in this picture, isn't there?
   Sue's dad: a) Yes, you were standing too far away.
   b) Yes, the camera is too small.
   c) Yes, May's too near the pond.

Now ask and answer.

Oh dear. Here's the pond, but where are the butterflies?

They're too small to see.

Teacher/parent note : In the first activity, pupils listen to a conversation and circle the correct answers. In the second activity, they practise the conversation in pairs.

 **Listening**

Listen and write.

Would you like to be a better photographer?
Photography Lessons

Mrs Yan is going to give photography lessons for 10 to 15 year olds.

Day: (1) <u>Every Wednesday</u>

Time: 5:30 p.m. to (2) _____

For: (3) _____ weeks

Starting on: (4) _____ July

Come and learn to:

- take pictures of (5) _____

- take pictures of animals, plants and the environment around you

- (8) _____ your pictures to your friends

- take pictures of (6) _____

- (7) _____ your pictures on your computer

- make your pictures more colourful

If you haven't got a camera, you can (9) _____ the school's camera.

Only (10) $ _____ for each lesson!

Read and draw lines.

1. If Sue goes to the lessons,
2. If Sue goes to the beach,
3. If you're 9 years old,
4. If you haven't got a camera,
5. If you want to take better pictures,

- you'll learn a lot at Mrs Yan's lessons.
- you're too young to go to the lessons.
- you can use the school's camera.
- she'll have to pay $4 each week.
- she'll take pictures of turtles and octopuses.

Teacher/parent note : Pupils revise the first conditional. In the first activity, they listen to a conversation and fill in the correct information. In the second activity, they match the beginnings of sentences with the correct endings.

💬 Speaking

Pretend to be Sue's mum. Why can't Sue go for photography lessons? Look at the pictures and say. Use the words in the boxes to help you.

visit aunt / take / to lessons

expensive

no-one / take home / from lessons

dad / use computer / work

On Wednesdays, I have to visit your aunt.
I can't take you to your lessons.

How can Sue solve the problems? Read and say. Use the words in the box.

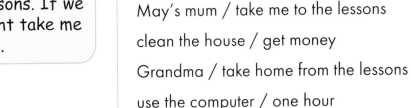

May is going for the lessons. If we ask May's mum, she might take me to the lessons.

May's mum / take me to the lessons

clean the house / get money

Grandma / take home from the lessons

use the computer / one hour

How else can Sue solve the problems?

Teacher/parent note : In the first activity, pupils look at the pictures and helping words to identify the problems. In the second activity, pupils use the helping words to suggest solutions to the problems. In the third activity, they suggest other ways to solve the problems.

Word List

Animals
butterfly	76
cricket	55
insects	55
octopus	46
swan	72
turtle	46

Clothes
belt	64
pocket	52
shorts	70
uniform	16

Countries, people and places around the world
Arctic	32
Indonesia	55
Korowai	30
London	70
New Zealand	33
Turkey	33

Family, friends and ourselves
adult	9
Alberto	32
Alfred	32
Anita	32
Betty	71
Claire	30
Ebenezer Scrooge	68
Ethan	34
Jacob Marley	68
Jeremy	55
Michael	71
Raj	32
Robert	74
Sahu	30
Sarah	74
Simon	64

Festivals
Christmas	68
Easter	64

Folklore and fantasy
believe	47
dream	47
future	18
ghost	68
secret	47
wish	60

Food and drink
chopsticks	64
dessert	26
doughnut/donut	52
fork	64
hot chocolate	60
marshmallow	60
meal	24
noodles	64
packet	50
peanut	70
pepper/capsicum	58
pizza	24
snack	80
sour	59
spoon	64
sweets/candy	38

Going for a holiday
comb	70
hostel	72
queue	70
shampoo	70
soap	70
suitcase	70
toothpaste	70
video camera	6

Homes
carpet	33
cooker	60
curtains	37
fridge	40
igloo	32
key	52
ladder	34

letterbox	52
toilet	30
tree house	30

Jobs and the world of work
actor	14
artist	6
business	33
chemist	12
detective	6
doctor	14
engineer	22
farmer	12
fireman	15
footballer	13
interview	6
job	12
journalist	6
mechanic	14
news	14
newspaper	14
photographer	8
pilot	14
policeman	14
postman	12
secretary	6
singer	20
tennis player	8
thief	10
waiter	62
writer	6

Other things
comment	24
illness	23
information	42
trolley	58

Patterns
spotted	46
striped	64

Places and directions

airport	72
college	76
corner	52
east	73
factory	12
fire station	15
front	11
north	73
office	12
police station	52
post office(box)	6
post office	12
south	72
studio	6
theatre	38
west	72

School and the classroom

air conditioner	40
envelope	6
ink	46
language	13
letter	6
meeting	40
problem	38
stamp	12
student	72
water cooler	40

Sports and play

adventure	33
clue	10
competition	6
footprints	10
health	22
idea	6
mystery	6
score (a goal)	13
(frog) tank	52
tape recorder	13

The school garden

bush	52
pond	76
shade	40
swing	76
umbrella	76

The senses

feel (like)	24
look (like)	24
smell (like)	24
sound (like)	26
taste (like)	24

The weather

fog	69
foggy	75
storm	30

The world around us

air	18
environment	46
rubbish	46
sky	30
smoke	15

Transport

fire engine	15
ship	48

What time is it?

a.m.	52
century	68
midday	52
midnight	52
p.m.	52
tonight	60

Action words (verbs)

act	14
agree	39
aren't	7
ask for	52

become	21
begin	55
belong	33
build	34
call	12
cost	40
decide	20
die	9
disturb	47
doesn't	7
fall (in love)	33
fetch	58
find out	52
finish	70
fix	14
float	46
follow	52
forget	10
happen	10
invite	26
lived	30
look after	55
look for	52
make	33
may	18
might	22
move in	30
plant	40
point	11
post	12
protect	15
scold	65
scream	48
sell	33
send	6
shot	46
should	36
sink	46
slip	46
solve	6
steal	38
study	22
touch	55
travel	22

turn off	65
use	64
wave	47
whisper	52
will	18
win	6
won't	18

Words that tell about action words (adverbs)

also	38
always	30
anymore	58
anywhere	12
away	72
else	11
everywhere	12
excitedly	9
hard	33
just (like)	10
nowhere	12
perhaps	18
really	9
rudely	69
safely	15
somewhere	12
soon	80
still	19
straight (on)	73
suddenly	46

Joining words (conjunctions)

if	55

Things we say (formulaic expressions)

excuse me	9
gosh	9
yours sincerely	6

Words that tell how many (determiners)

(a) few	71

enough	58
(a) little	71
(too) much	70
(too) many	70

Words that tell more about people/things (adjectives)

bored	9
burning	15
burnt	60
busy	73
cheap	58
clear	48
closed	52
colourful	33
comfortable	37
deep	30
delicious	36
empty	52
excellent	6
expensive	58
extinct	47
famous	6
fantastic	88
free	72
fresh	24
full (of)	62
hard	59
healthy	24
heavy	58
high	58
important	11
longest	32
lovely	24
low	59
missing	52
other	20
perfect	60
poor	68
ready	55
real	15
rich	13
same	21

shiny	46
shortest	32
sick	9
slippery	55
softest	29
soggy	60
special	55
sure	12
surprised	9
unkind	69

Words that tell where things are (prepositions)

since	30
through	53
until	33
without	60

Words to talk about people and things (pronouns)

anyone	12
anything	12
each	72
everyone	12
everything	12
no-one	12
nothing	13
someone	12
something	12

Now I know 305 more words! Fantastic!